BUGS! BUGS! BUGS!

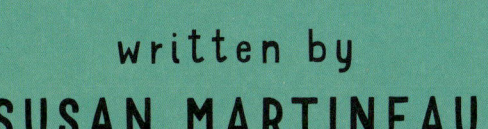

b small

written by
SUSAN MARTINEAU

illustrated by
VICKY BARKER

For Steve, who always gets the spiders out of the bath for me! - S.M

For Olive, and the spider in her playhouse. - V.B

b small

Published by b small publishing ltd.
Station House, Station Approach,
East Horsley, Leatherhead,
KT24 6QX, UK
www.bsmall.co.uk

Text and illustrations copyright © b small publishing ltd. 2025

1 2 3 4 5   ISBN 978-1-916851-25-2

Publisher: Sam Hutchinson. Creative director: Vicky Barker.

Printed in China by WKT Co. Ltd. on FSC-certified paper, supporting responsible forestry.

All rights reserved.

No reproduction, copy or transmission of this publication may be made without written permission. No part of this publication may be reproduced, stored in a retrieval system or transmitted in any form or by any means, electronic, mechanical, photocopying, recording or otherwise, without the prior permission of the publisher.

British Library Cataloguing-in-Publication Data.
A catalogue record for this book is available from the British Library.
To contact our Authorised Representative within the EU, please visit: bsmall.co.uk/EUregulations
Batch code: 202505WKT

Contents

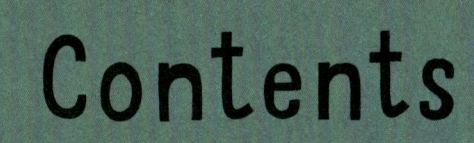

4-5	Welcome to bug world	20-21	Buzzing around
6-7	Brilliant beetles	22-23	Silky superpowers
8-9	Munching and slurping	24-25	Record-breakers!
10-11	Minibeast babies	26-27	Wriggly and slimy
12-13	In disguise!	28-29	Water bugs
14-15	Winged wonders	30-31	A buggy nuisance!
16-17	At home with ants	32-33	We need bugs!
18-19	Super senses	34-35	Special bug words

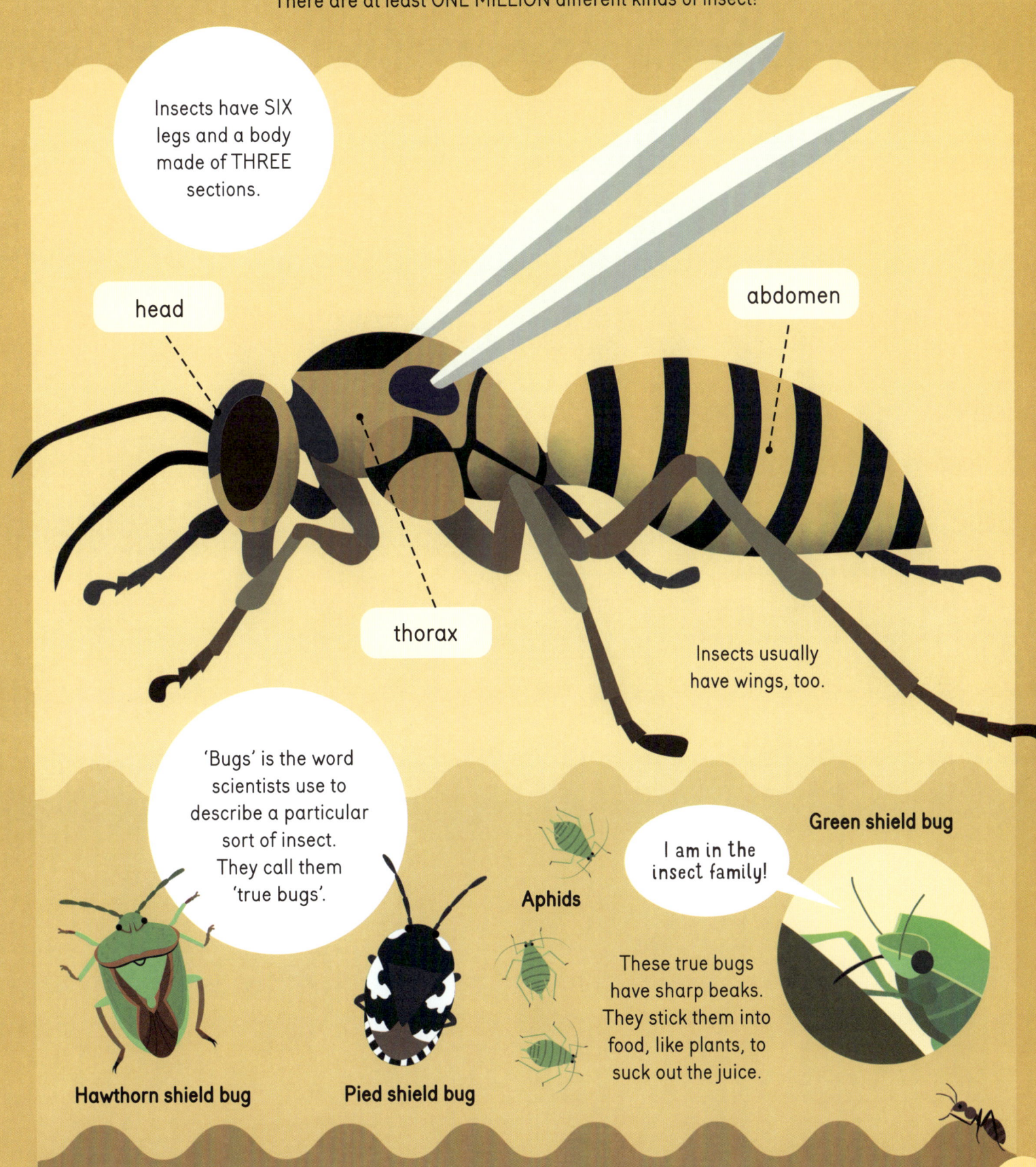

Brilliant beetles

Beetles are insects. These amazing creatures live all over the world. They are many different shapes, sizes and colours.

More than 400,000 types of beetle have been discovered so far.

Beetles have hard wing cases. These protect the beetle's flying wings that are underneath. Some of these wing cases are very beautiful.

The **rainbow leaf beetle** is very rare and lives mainly in mountain forests.

Rose chafers are **iridescent** green beetles with a V shape where their wings meet.

Rosemary beetles have shiny stripes of green and reddish-purple. These small beetles eat the leaves of herb plants.

Titan beetles can be over 16 cm long. They have the longest body of any beetle. They live in the hot jungles of South America.

The **bombardier beetle** has a secret weapon to fight off **predators**. It can shoot a blast of boiling hot liquid out of its bottom!

Whoosh!

Stag beetles are fierce fighters. They use their massive jaws to fight other **stag beetles** and to attract a mate.

Glow-worms are beetles, not worms! The female beetle glows with a yellow-green light to attract a mate.

Ladybirds are small beetles with beautiful spots and colours. These put off **predators** looking for a snack.

Munching and slurping

Bugs eat all kinds of things. Some only eat plants, some eat other bugs! There are also bugs that eat stuff like wood, dead animals and poo.

Beetles and ants have strong jaws. These are handy for chomping tough leaves and catching **prey**.

Trap-jaw ants have one of the snappiest bites around!

True bugs suck up their food. **Green shield bugs** feed on tree sap.

Slurp!

Butterflies drink a sweet liquid called **nectar** from flowers using a tube called a **proboscis**. It is like a long and pointy straw that butterflies can curl up under their heads.

8

The **praying mantis** has strong jaws and long front legs with spikes. It keeps very, very still and just moves its beady eyes until it is ready to snatch its food!

Mosquitoes and **fleas** feed on the blood of animals. Their mouthparts are like needles.

Houseflies have tongues like mops at the end of tubes. They use these to soak up liquids. They can also make solid food into liquid by squirting out juices through these tubes.

Some bugs, like **dung beetles**, are **scavengers**. They eat dead animals and poo. They do a good job of tidying up!

Termites, and some beetles, like chomping through wood. They can really damage wooden buildings.

9

Minibeast babies

Baby bugs grow in different ways. Some of them go through many stages between being an egg and an adult minibeast. Other bug babies hatch out looking just like their parents.

Butterflies, moths, beetles, bees and flies are insects that go through FOUR stages to become an adult.

Butterfly babies

1. Eggs are laid on leaves.

2. Caterpillars (**larvae**) hatch out and start munching leaves. The **larvae** shed their skin several times as they get bigger.

3. Their skin turns into a shell and the caterpillars turn into **pupae**.

4. The **pupae** open and out come brand-new butterflies.

Grasshoppers, crickets, damselflies, dragonflies, and true bugs are insects that go through THREE stages to become an adult.

Grasshopper babies

1. Eggs are laid in soil.

2. Tiny **nymphs** hatch out. They shed their skin several times as they grow. They look a bit like adult grasshoppers, with six legs but no wings.

3. Finally, their skin splits and out come adult grasshoppers with wings.

In disguise!

Many bugs can fly away from danger, but it can be handy for them to become invisible instead, or to make themselves look like something else!

Some minibeasts have colours and patterns to help them **camouflage**. This means they blend into where they live.

Some bugs pretend not to be bugs! They **camouflage** themselves to look like bark, lichen, sticks or stones.

Waved umber moth caterpillars look just like twigs. They keep completely still when a **predator** is nearby.

The **garden carpet moth** spreads its wings out as it rests on a wall.

The **early thorn moth** caterpillar also resembles a twig during the day. At night it wriggles off to find food. When it becomes an adult moth, it looks just like dead leaves!

Winged wonders

Butterflies and moths are some of the most beautiful flying insects on Earth. Their amazing wings are made of thousands of teeny, overlapping scales.

Butterflies are out and about during the day.

Butterflies rest with their wings folded upwards.

Monarch butterflies travel thousands of kilometres between Mexico and Canada every year.

The dazzling **blue morpho butterfly** lives in the rainforests of Central and South America.

Red admiral butterflies will chase off other butterflies to defend their territory!

The family of **swallowtail butterflies** includes some of the largest and most colourful butterflies in the world.

14

Moths are mainly **nocturnal** and come out at night.

Moths rest with their wings open and flat.

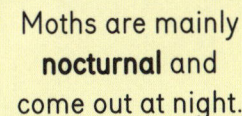

Moths are cold-blooded, like all insects. At night, when there is no sun to warm them up, the moths have to quiver their wings before they take off.

Moths have different **antennae**, or feelers, to butterflies. They are shorter and feathery.

A moth's **antennae** can detect the scent of other moths from kilometres away.

moth

butterfly

The **atlas moth** from Asia is massive! It can be up to 25 cm from wing tip to wing tip.

25 cm

The **garden tiger moth** rubs its wings together to make a hissing sound. This frightens off **predators**.

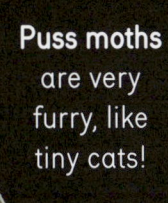

Puss moths are very furry, like tiny cats!

15

At home with ants

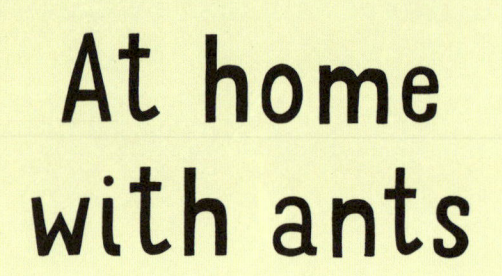

Ants live in enormous groups in large underground nests. These are called **colonies**. There might be thousands, or even millions, of ants in one **colony**.

There is a queen ant and lots of worker ants.

Worker ants have different jobs in the **colony**.

They keep the nest clean. They can even make sure it is not too hot or cold by opening or closing passageways.

They go out to look for food and lay a scent trail to guide other ants to it. This means they don't get lost on the way home either.

Oi! It's this way!

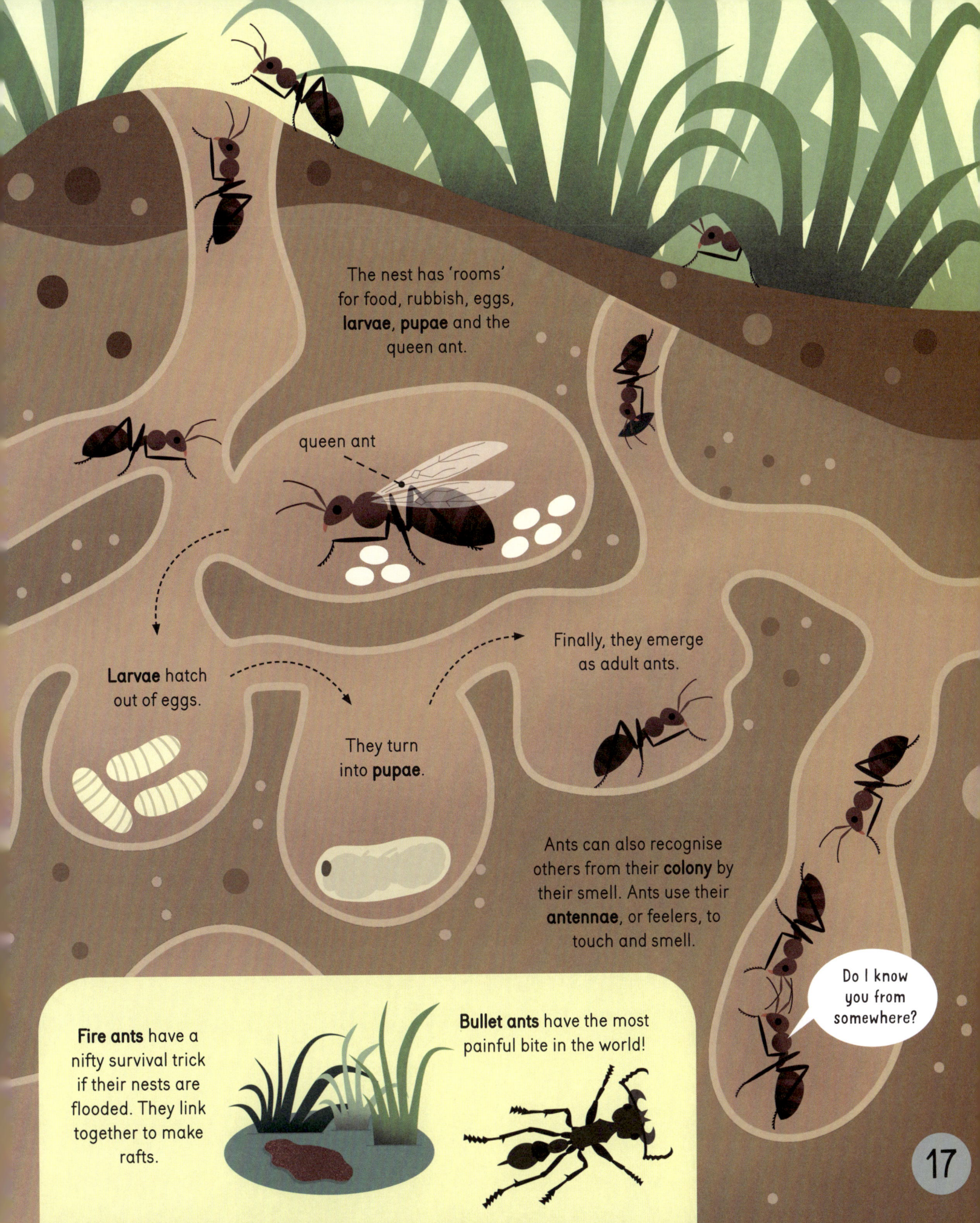

Super senses

Bugs use their senses of sight, smell, touch, taste and hearing to find food and to stay safe from danger. Their senses are very different to ours.

Many bugs have **antennae**, or feelers. They don't just use them to feel things though. They also use them to smell and taste as they explore their surroundings and hunt for food.

Antennae can be long, short, straight or bendy!

The **cockchafer beetle** has fan-like **antennae**. These spread out to sense smells in the air.

Common wasps are brilliant smellers! They use their **antennae** to detect all kinds of leftovers as well as other bugs to eat.

Ooh, yummy!

Some insects, like butterflies and flies, taste things with their feet.

18

Buzzing around

There are thousands of different kinds of bee in the world. **Honeybees** live together in groups called **colonies** and they have very busy lives!

Each **honeybee colony** has a queen. She is the largest bee.

There are thousands of worker bees in a **colony**.

Worker bees make wax in their bodies. They use it to build six-sided shapes called cells.

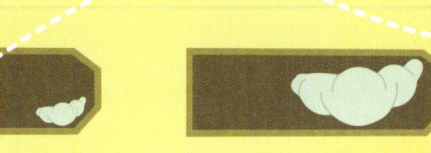

1. The queen lays eggs in the cells.

2. They hatch into grubs (**larvae**).

3. The grubs grow and grow.

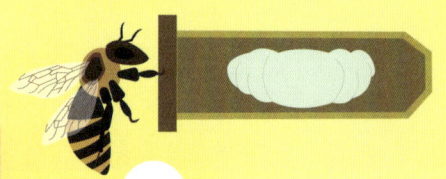

4. When they are big enough, the worker bees plug the cells with wax.

5. The **larvae** turn into **pupae**. Inside these cocoons they grow legs, eyes and wings.

6. The grown-up bees chew their way out and join the **colony**.

20

Bees spread **pollen** from flower to flower as they collect food. This helps the plants to form seeds or fruits. This is called **pollination**.

Honeybees have long tongues covered in hairs. They stretch them through their tube-like mouths to suck out **nectar**.

Worker bees gather **nectar** and **pollen** from flowers. They make honey from the **nectar**. They feed honey and **pollen** to the little grubs.

When a worker bee finds some **nectar**, it goes back to the hive to let other bees know where it is by doing a special dance. This tells the other bees where to find the food.

It's not far!

21

Silky superpowers

Spiders are not insects. They are **arachnids**. Their bodies are in two parts. They have eight legs, but no wings or **antennae**. Most of them have eight eyes, too!

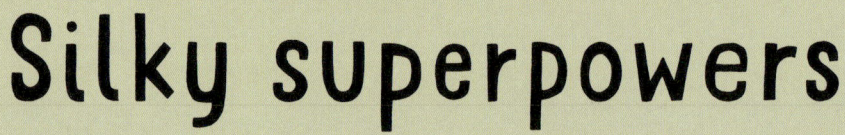

And we've got FANGS!

Spiders have an amazing superpower. They can make silk from special glands inside their bodies. It is stronger than steel wire of the same thickness.

Spiders use their silk in many different ways.

Garden spiders make beautiful orb webs where they hang head down waiting for **prey** to get caught in the sticky threads.

Spiders bite their **prey** with a venom which kills them. Then they wrap it up in a silk parcel to eat later.

House spiders spin cobwebs in corners. These are like dense mats to trap insects.

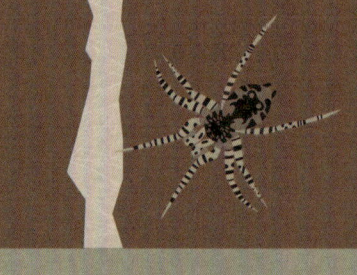

Wall spiders make tube-like webs in cracks in the wall. These have a tripwire to let the spider know when dinner has arrived!

Record-breakers!

There really are some amazing bugs out there! Here are some of the fastest, biggest, jumpiest, strongest and most amazing of them all.

The heftiest spider is the **South American Goliath birdeater**.

This chunky beast has a leg span of up to 30 cm and weighs 175 g. That's around the size of a large dinner plate and as heavy as a big, juicy apple!

Tiger beetles are the fastest insects on land. The **Australian tiger beetle** can zip along at 9 kilometres an hour. That is like a human running at about 800 kph!

The longest **stick insect** found in the wild measured over 62 cm.

I am hard to spot, too!

The **diabolical ironclad beetle** can survive being run over by a car! Its wing cases have pieces that lock together to make it super-hero tough.

Weeeeeeeeeeeeee!

Sharpshooters are true bugs. They feed on the sap of plants and have to suck up a lot to keep themselves going. This makes so much wee that they catapult it away from their bums at high speed!

The **common froghopper** is only 6 mm long, but it can jump 70 cm into the air. That is like a human leaping over a tower block!

The world's strongest insect for its size is a **horned dung beetle**. It can pull such a heavy weight that it is like a human lifting six full double-decker buses!

Hey! Keep the noise down!

Giant cicadas are probably the loudest bugs around! Their drumming noise can be heard 1.6 kilometres away.

25

Wriggly and slimy

These creepy crawlies are not insects. Some of them have hundreds of legs and others use slime to get around.

Millipedes and centipedes are **myriapods**. This means 'many-legged'.

Millipedes have two pairs of legs on each segment of their bodies. Some millipedes can have as many as 750 legs!

Round body and short **antennae**.

Millipedes crawl about in damp places under leaves. They are **herbivores** and eat rotting plants.

The **giant African millipede** can grow over 30 cm long.

Centipedes have one pair of legs on each segment of their body. Centipedes can have more than 350 legs.

Flat body and long **antennae**.

Centipedes are **carnivores** and eat other creatures. They run very fast and have poisonous claws on their heads to kill small insects, worms and millipedes!

Water bugs

Ponds and streams are good places for bugs to live. There is usually lots of food for them, and safe places to hide and to begin their lives.

Whirligig beetles spin on the surface of the water. Their eyes are in two parts. One part looks under the water and the other looks up.

eye looking up

eye looking down

I'm getting dizzy!

Pond skaters have special waterproof hairs on their feet. This helps them move about on the water surface. They row across the water with their long, thin back and middle legs.

Diving beetles, like the **great diving beetle**, have flatter bodies than land beetles to help them swim better. They can also trap air bubbles under their wings so they can breathe under the water.

28

A buggy nuisance!

Some bugs and minibeasts can be a terrible pest. They spread nasty illnesses or damage crops that humans need.

Mosquitoes have a tube-like mouth (**proboscis**) which they use to bite and to suck blood from animals, including humans.

Only female **mosquitoes** bite. Sometimes **mosquitoes** can pass on dangerous diseases like malaria, yellow fever, dengue and Zika virus.

Aphids, caterpillars and other hungry bugs munch their way through plants that humans need for food and wood we need for building.

In some countries vast swarms of **desert locusts** can eat through fields of crops in just a few hours. This leaves farmers without food or anything to sell to look after their families.

Chemicals called pesticides are often used to get rid of pesky minibeasts. But these chemicals don't just kill the pests. They can also harm humans, other wildlife and our environment.

Pesticides can also hurt the bugs that we really need to keep a healthy balance of life on our planet. We need to use less harmful ways to control the pests.

Some bugs like to live ON us!

Head lice can be a really annoying pest! But you don't need chemicals to get rid of them. Just a very fine comb!

Ladybirds and most kinds of wasp are very helpful **predators**. They like to eat the bugs that destroy crops and trees.

Put those chemicals down!

My head is itchy!

We need bugs!

Bugs have been on our planet for hundreds of millions of years. They were here before the dinosaurs. They are an essential part of life on Earth.

We are pollinators ...

Insects carry **pollen** from flower to flower as they feed on **nectar**. This helps plants make more seeds. These seeds grow into new plants, including the ones we and other animals need for food.

Bees, wasps, hoverflies, beetles, butterflies and moths are all essential **pollinators**. All other creatures, including humans, could not survive without them.

We are food ...

Bugs are very important as food for lots of bigger creatures. Sometimes bugs even eat each other!

Humans also eat bugs in many countries. They may be a very useful kind of food for us all in the future.

32

We are cleaners and recyclers ...

Bugs eat dead and rotting stuff. As they do this it breaks it into smaller bits which feeds the soil and makes it healthy. This helps trees and plants to grow.

BUT bugs are in danger!

We need your help!

Humans have made life very difficult for bugs. We have chopped down forests, put damaging chemicals into our world and changed the climate. This makes it hard for bugs to find the food and homes they need.

Perhaps you would like to be a scientist who studies bugs when you grow up? You could start now in your garden or local park. Be an **entomologist**!

If you have a garden or outside area you could find out about the best plants to attract **pollinators**. You could build a bug hotel!

33

Special bug words

Annelid is the scientific name for an animal with a body made up of segments. Earthworms are annelids.

Antennae are the feelers on a minibeast's head. They use them for touching, smelling and tasting.

Arachnid has no antennae or wings. It has eight legs. Spiders are arachnids.

Camouflage is the way the shape or colour of a creature helps it to blend into its surroundings.

Carnivore is an animal that hunts and eats other animals.

Colony is a large number of the same kind of creature living in one big group.

Entomologist is a scientist who studies minibeasts.

Gastropod is the scientific name for slugs and snails.

Herbivore is an animal that eats plants.

Invertebrate is an animal without a backbone (spine).

Iridescent means bright colours that seem to shimmer and change.

Larvae are insects in the stage after hatching from eggs.

Lenses are the parts inside eyes that help animals to see clearly.

Mimic is when a creature pretends to be something else to protect itself or to find prey.

Myriapod is the scientific name for minibeasts with many legs, like millipedes and centipedes.

Nectar is sweet liquid made by many flowers.

Nocturnal describes a creature that is active at night.

Nymphs are young insects that do not change into pupae before they become adults.

Pollen is powder made by flowers so that they can make seeds to grow new plants.

Pollination is when pollen is spread from flower to flower. This means plants can make more seeds and fruit.

Pollinators are animals, like insects, that spread pollen.

34

Predator is an animal that hunts other animals to eat.

Prey are the creatures that predators like to hunt and eat.

Proboscis is a long, tube-like tongue.

Pupae are insects in the stage between being larvae and adults.

Scavenger means a creature that eats things that are already dead.